3 Amazing Miracles When My Mom Died

A True Story of a Catholic Family Who Witnessed 3 Amazing Miracles When Their Mother Died and Came Back to Life!

"A beautiful story that will inspire you to seek a love to leave heaven for!"

"PASSING ON THE ANCHOR THAT KEPT ME STANDING— TRUE STORIES THAT COULD SAVE YOU."

MIRACLE ANCHOR LLC

Copyright

3 Amazing Miracles When My Mom Died

A True Story of a Catholic Family Who Witnessed 3 Amazing Miracles When Their Mother Passed Away and Came Back to Life

Copyright © 2025 by Miracle Anchor LLC

All rights reserved.

No part of this book may be reproduced, stored in a retrieval system, or transmitted in any form or by any means—electronic, mechanical, photocopying, recording, or otherwise—without the prior written permission of the publisher, except for brief quotations used in reviews, articles, or other critical works.

For information, inquiries, or permissions, please contact:
Miracle Anchor LLC, Sheridan, WY 82801
Email: info@miracleanchor.com
Website: https://miracleanchor.com/

This book is an accurate account of somebody's daughter's personal experiences and reflections. Illustrations will be labeled if not the original. Most names have not been included for privacy and security reasons. If you would like to know more information, reach out to us as we may be able to provide depending on its purpose.

Cover Design and Illustrations Created with the assistance of AI Tools: Grok from xAI, Canva, Chat GPT.
ISBN: 979-8-9937425-0-2
Printed in the United States of America.

"Love never dies, for it is born of Heaven."

Dedication

To a beautiful mother-Sharon, who represented love —
may the love & miracles you gave us be shared with The
World, until we meet again.

MIRACLE
ANCHOR LLC

Preface

In this book, I share the experiences that kept me anchored through life's hardest storms. These pages were written to help others find strength and clarity when the waves rise. My hope is that my Journey brings comfort, hope, and courage to yours.

A Journey of Faith, Family, and Miracles.

TABLE OF CONTENTS

Description   **Page**

PART I: THE SEEDS OF LOVE AND FAITH

A Humble Beginning in Iowa — 02
Where faith and family took root on the "wrong side of the tracks."

A Young Heart Tested by Love — 04
The heartbreak that shaped her trust in God's greater plan.

A Mother's Courage — 06
Choosing life, love, and faith over fear.

A Dance of Destiny — 08
The providence of two souls—when God wrote their love story.

A Family Forged in Faith — 10
Building a home where prayer was the foundation and love was the roof.

PART II: A LIFE POURED OUT IN LOVE

A Mother's Gentle Touch — 14
The quiet strength and tender grace that filled every corner of our home.

A New Chapter by the Lake — 16
A Season of reflection, peace, and love renewed by the water's edge.

A Heartbreaking Diagnosis — 18
When faith was tested and courage became her song.

Preparing for a Family's Vigil — 20
The sacred waiting—surrounded by faith, prayer, and love.

Dedication

To my beautiful mother — Sharon
whose love was constant, whose heart was our home,
and whose gentle strength carried us through every storm.
Thank you for always being there, for every sacrifice, every
prayer, and every moment of unconditional love.
Your light still guides us, and your love lives on in all we do.

MIRACLE
ANCHOR LLC

TABLE OF CONTENTS

Description   **Page**

PART III: Heaven Draws Near

When Darkness Deepened, Heaven Stirred — 22
The threshold between earth and eternity begins to open.

The First Miracle: Heaven's Thunder — 23
When our hymns reached Heaven, God answered through the storm.

My Dad Who Spoke Straight Lines — 25
The steadfast faith and quiet strength of a husband and father.

The Second Miracle: The Touch of Heaven's Gate — 27
"Are you going to let me in?" — the moment Heaven opened its door.

A Farewell in Her Hometown— The Visitor No One Expected — 28
Love remembered, even by the one who once walked away decades earlier.

The Third Miracle: A Return of Faithful Love — 30
When love crossed Heaven's gate to comfort one last time.

Dedication

To my courageous mother — Sharon,
who chose life when the world told her not to,
who faced judgment with grace, and heartbreak with faith.
You believed in God's plan when others could not see it,
and through your strength, love was born.
Your courage became our foundation,
and your faith turned shame into a story of redemption and hope.

TABLE OF CONTENTS

| **Description** | **Page** |

PART IV: The Light That Remains

What My Mom Taught Me About the Power of Prayer and Faith — 33
Lessons of devotion, sacrifice, and the eternal promise of God's love.

Thoughts and Miracle Meanings I Have Reflected Upon — 36
Reflections on Heaven's signs — and finding a love worth leaving Heaven for.

Prayers We Were Taught — 39

PART I

The Seeds of Love and Faith

A Humble Beginning in Iowa

Where Faith and Family Took Root on the "Wrong Side of the Tracks."

Iowa,
United States
1946

In the gentle embrace of a small Iowa town, where the population numbered fewer than 3,000 souls, my mother came into the world in July 1946. Born as a twin, she and her sister were the youngest of six children—five girls and one boy—to devoted parents who labored tirelessly at the local factory.

Their cozy home, nestled on what some whispered was "the wrong side of the tracks," was a haven of love amid modest means.

Raised in the warm light of the Lutheran faith, my mother grew up in a close-knit family, where strict but loving rules guided their days. They played joyful games by the creek, diligently shared chores, and held fast to the values of obedience and kindness. Faith was the cornerstone of their lives.

Her father, a stern yet caring man who enjoyed a drink now and then, led with firmness, ensuring no shadow of abuse or excess dimmed their strong, loving bond.

Despite their financial struggles, the family's basic needs were met, and love overflowed in abundance.

A house much like my mom's childhood home, where six of them lived together.

(Created with Grok by xAI.)

A Young Heart Tested by Love

The Heartbreak That Shaped Her Trust in God's Greater Plan.

My mother's youth was not without heartbreak. As a teenager, she fell deeply in love with a boy from a neighboring town. Their dreams seemed so bright, until his parents intervened, insisting he marry another girl they had chosen, threatening to cut him from their family will if he wed someone from humble origins.

Heartbroken, he chose the path of inheritance, choosing wealth over love, leaving my mother to carry the weight of a broken heart. Yet, her faith sustained her, and she pressed forward, trusting God's plan.

She graduated from high school in 1964, spent a brief time at a community college, and then bravely ventured to Washington, D.C., where she worked for the FBI for about a year. In that bustling capital, with its smoky social circles, she was introduced to cigarettes – a habit she later abandoned.

A family tale recounts a moment when she followed someone into a bathroom for surveillance, which ultimately sealed her decision to return home. There, in the familiar rhythm of small-town life, she trusted God's guiding hand.

This image is a mockup created for illustrative purposes, depicting my mother, an FBI agent, in a bathroom surveillance scenario.

(Created with Grok by xAI.)

A Mother's Courage

Choosing Life, Love, and Faith Over Fear.

In her early twenties, my mother found love again with a man from a town an hour away. Their time together led to an unexpected pregnancy.

The man, tied to a family in real estate, offered money for an abortion to wash their hands of the child.

My mother, with her deep faith, a heart rooted in love for life, and an upbringing in a family that cherished babies and children, stood firm—abortion was never an option. The family gave her a few hundred dollars and vanished from her life forever.

Undaunted, she chose to bring her daughter into the world, embracing single motherhood with courage and grace.

This beautiful girl became a testament to my mother's conviction with unwavering love and trust in God's plan.

This image is a mockup created for illustrative purposes, depicting my mother, pregnant, with a few hundred dollars from the young man to wash his hands of the child.

(Created with Grok by xAI.)

A Dance of Destiny

The Providence of Two Souls— When God Wrote Their Love Story.

A year or two later, destiny waltzed in at a dance hall an hour from her hometown, where my mother met my father.

A man of steadfast Catholic faith. Raised in a strict yet loving family, he attended the local Catholic school while his father delivered mail at the post office and his mother worked at a greenhouse. Their home, too, knew modest means, but love kept the lights on.

As a young child, my father spent time in foster-like care with a wonderful woman he adored when his mother needed help.

In grade school, he returned fully to his parents' care alongside a stepbrother ten years older. After high school, he served as an Air Force mechanic in Vietnam, enduring the heartbreaking loss of his best friend.

Despite his mother's objections to marrying a woman with a child, my father's love for my mother and her little girl was unshakeable. In 1971, they wed in a Catholic ceremony, embracing her new faith with devotion.

My father adopted her daughter immediately, and though tensions lingered with his family for years, their bond grew stronger.. Settling in the small town, my parents worked factory jobs, building a life hand in hand.

This image is of my parents wedding and the Catholic Church.

A Family Forged in Faith

Building a Home Where Prayer Was the Foundation and Love Was the Roof!

Eight years on, our family had grown to four children—three girls and one boy—cherishing every moment amid tight finances. Life was not easy; my parents labored tirelessly, my father running a junkyard and my mother serving as a medical secretary and, briefly, as a factory worker soldering metal.

Yet, her true calling was a homemaker, wife, and mother. With unwavering dedication, she nurtured her family, ensuring meals were on the table, the home was filled with love, and faith was ever-present.

One stormy night, lightning sparked a fire in our home's tunnel-shaped attic, engulfing the upstairs where we children would be asleep.

Miraculously, no one was sleeping, but my mother was told we would have perished if asleep. This shook her deeply, becoming her turning point toward deeper faith. She began teaching Catholic catechism weekly, reading scripture books, hanging a rosary on the wall, placing a Bible on the coffee table, and adorning our home with statues from the old Catholic school.

One evening, returning from the factory, she heard us children say grace before dinner and asked my father when we learned it. In that moment, she declared, "That's it, I'm done with the factory," choosing to be a stay-at-home mom, to pour her heart thoroughly into her family, becoming a soft place to land for her children.

My father started the junkyard outside on our few acres, working long hours, while my mother kept our world inside, loving and orderly. She was our room mother at school, volunteered at church, celebrated every birthday and holiday with warmth, and ensured a home-cooked meal every day.

When we fell ill, she whisked us to the doctor, joking she'd visited so often she could own the place. She rarely left home at night, never partied or drank, devoting her days to cooking, cleaning, helping Dad, and chatting on the phone with loved ones.

My father expanded our five-acre haven with cattle, hogs, horses, dogs, and cats, even buying a livestock sale barn that we ran for a year before selling it. Bank visits made him nervous—the only time I saw him so—dressing up in his finest clothes to ask for extensions.

My father always paid his debts. Once, a legal dispute arose over a scrap-metal contract with my mother's old teenage love—the one who chose to keep his name in the family will—but it settled in our favor.

My parents seldom argued in front of us, and our life was one of hard work and simple joys. As children, we helped in the junkyard, cutting stems from inner tubes for recycling, and then celebrating a full semi-load with a rare pizza. We ate out sparingly, learning hard work from Dad after school until sunset. Sundays were sacred: church and family meals with Grandma.

PART II
A Life Poured Out in Love

When we fell ill, she whisked us to the doctor, joking she'd visited so often she could own the place. She rarely left home at night, never partied or drank, devoting her days to cooking, cleaning, helping Dad, and chatting on the phone with loved ones.

My father expanded our five-acre haven with cattle, hogs, horses, dogs, and cats, even buying a livestock sale barn that we ran for a year before selling it. Bank visits made him nervous—the only time I saw him so—dressing up in his finest clothes to ask for extensions.
My father always paid his debts. Once, a legal dispute arose over a scrap-metal contract with my mother's old teenage love—the one who chose to keep his name in the family will—but it settled in our favor.

My parents seldom argued in front of us, and our life was one of hard work and simple joys. As children, we helped in the junkyard, cutting stems from inner tubes for recycling, and then celebrating a full semi-load with a rare pizza. We ate out sparingly, learning hard work from Dad after school until sunset. Sundays were sacred: church and family meals with Grandma.

PART II
A Life Poured Out in Love

A Mother's Gentle Touch

The Quiet Strength and Tender Grace That Filled Every Corner of Our Home.

My mother's love was a soft, enduring glow. She lived in our small town for 32 years, helping Dad. She was a devoted member of the local Catholic church, where she taught elementary catechism for years.

Her greatest passion? Her family. She selflessly sacrificed her gifts for us, friends, and the community, engaging in heartfelt conversations with anyone, listening deeply, and making each person feel special. She knew us children better than we knew ourselves.

Her joys were simple: music, drawing, kitchen dances to country tunes, birds, flowers, warm scented candles, autumn's hues,

Christmas lights and festivities, games, toys, dolls, baking, and fishing with Dad, and most of all, her eight grandchildren.

Patient, wise, caring, and understanding, she was our "soft place to land."

Truly, she was love Incarnate.

A New Chapter by the Lake

A Season of Reflection, Peace, and Love Renewed by the Water's Edge.

By 1995, they were empty nesters, with all children graduating from college—three girls marrying and starting families, the boy remaining single.

In 2002-2003, a car accident shook us: an older driver ran a stop sign, hitting Mom at 60 mph, rolling her car into a ditch. Miraculously, she walked out hours later with leg scars; after that, driving became rare for her.

Dad chose not to sue, grateful for the insurance that covered costs and left a bit extra—they were simply thankful she lived.

In 2004, with no retirement savings from prioritizing family, I bought their scrap business.

They moved hours away to a lakeside home, a place for long-overdue dates and quiet time together. I planted a flower garden like our old one, with her favorites, including the Burning Bush, to make it feel like home as she left behind friends and family.

We all believed this would be their golden chapter, free from the junkyard's constant interruptions. Not realizing we would only have around three more years.

This is part of the actual flower garden after over a decade of her passing.

A Heartbreaking Diagnosis

When Faith was tested and courage became her song.

In 2006, feeling unwell, my sister and I gently urged Mom to a doctor's appointment an hour away.

Tests and X-rays revealed pulmonary fibrosis, a merciless lung disease where tissue scars and stiffens, making breathing harder over time. Like hardened lungs, it worsens variably, with no cure in 2006 or today.

Doctors couldn't pinpoint the cause; Though its cause remained a mystery—perhaps linked to her brief time in a soldering fume-filled factory room—my mother faced it with courage.

The grim prognosis—six months to a year—no cure, changed everything. She quit smoking immediately, like she would when she was pregnant, though it wasn't the direct cause.

Our faithful mother, who loved Jesus, Mary, and Joseph, taught catechism and prayers, devoted her life to us and Dad, cherished board games, painting, singing, drawing, cooking, music, candles, flowers, holidays, birthdays, and grandchildren, and was slipping away too soon.

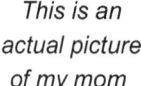
This is an actual picture of my mom

Preparing for a Family's Vigil

The Sacred Waiting—
Surrounded by Faith, Prayer, and Love.

Scattered hours or states away with our own families, we visited more, staying connected via calls and an electronic tablet for games and chats as She became bedridden.

She wished to pass at home, avoiding hospitals or nursing homes. Dad cared for her devotedly for months, her sisters rotating weekends.

Her last Christmas—once filled with perfect decorations, music, wrapped gifts, baked cookies, and church attire—was spent in bed, less mobile, tiring quickly on oxygen, with Dad tenderly upholding traditions.

PART III
Heaven Draws Near

When Darkness Deepened, Heaven Stirred

The Threshold Between Earth and Eternity Begins to Open.

In her final weeks, bedridden with hospice, we children and sisters took shifts. Her oxygen depleting, dependence worried me—I slept on the floor to ensure the breathing tube stayed in, despite Dad's protests.

When she stopped eating, we knew days remained.

Then, the divine miracles unfolded, testaments to the love and grace that defined her life.

The First Miracle: Heaven's Thunder

When Our Hymns Reached Heaven, God Answered Through the Storm.

Days before, eyes rarely open and words few, we four children gathered by her bed. I suggested singing our childhood church hymns—like
"Let There Be Peace on Earth,"
"Amazing Grace,"
"Hail Mary, Gentle Woman," and others—to comfort her. The three sisters sang joyfully; our brother, no singer, hesitated.

    As our voices rose in harmony a few songs in, a thunderous rumble shook the closet for about 30 seconds.

We continued, wide-eyed, and even my brother joined in. A sacred reminder of God's presence.

My mother, stirred by the noise, asked for quiet, but we knew Heaven had joined our chorus. Dad, in another room watching TV, confirmed no earthly cause.

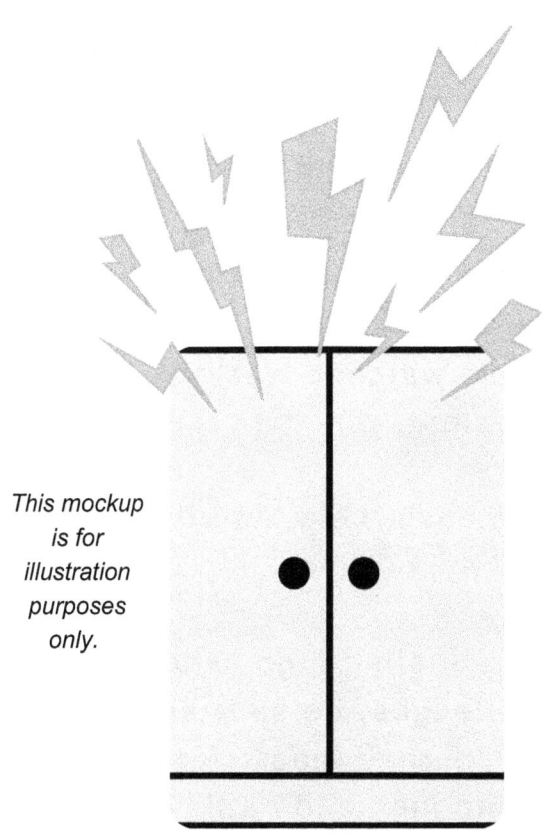

This mockup is for illustration purposes only.

My Dad Who Spoke Straight Lines

The Steadfast Faith and Quiet Strength of a Husband and Father.

To understand my father: A quiet man in his late 50s, direct and unsociable. He worked dawn to dusk, watched war or Western shows, and slept.

Short on cash, he'd load iron at 3 a.m. His life was work, Mom, then us kids.

Barely graduating high school due to reading challenges, he self-taught via the Wall Street Journal, mastering welding, fixing things, selling junk and cattle, and even creating a fishing tips pamphlet.

He inspired entrepreneurship and honesty, bluntly sharing opinions—like preferring Mom's old haircut. No cartoons on Saturdays; work called. He rarely said
"I love you," growing up,
but as a grandfather post-Mom, he softened.

Factual and to-the-point, he'd lock fighting siblings in the bathroom to pray until peace reigned.

This image is an AI generated picture of a junkyard used for illustrational purposes only.

(Created with Grok by xAI.)

The Second Miracle: The Touch of Heaven's Gate

"Are You Going to Let Me In?" the moment Heaven opened its door.

Hours before passing, eyes shut and silent, Mom spoke,
 "Are you going to let me in?"
She raised her arm, swaying as if opening a gate, then rested.

   Soon after, she passed into eternity. This moment—a glimpse of Heaven's gate—when her soul was welcomed home before her body rested —was a divine assurance of her eternal peace.

This AI image illustrates the swaying of a gate which my mom motioned versus a door handle.

(Created with Magic Media by Canva)

A Farewell in Her Hometown—The Visitor No One Expected

Love Remembered Even by the One Who Once Walked Away Decades Earlier.

Dad, preparing from months of caregiving, finished planning her funeral. She passed on Friday, sparing a child's Wednesday birthday as she had wished.

My mother's funeral in her hometown was a celebration of her life, attended by those who knew her warmth and grace.

Among them was an unexpected visitor—the man who had broken her heart in youth, paying his respects in silence, a poignant reminder of her journey through love and loss.

We held a Monday visitation, an evening vigil, and Tuesday was the burial. At the visitation, beside Dad near the casket, familiar faces paid their respects.

Then, a tailored man her age approached the casket, bowed his head for a minute, and left. Dad revealed it was her teenage love, saying goodbye. The man who chose to remain in the family will, over love, have visited the other side of the tracks one last time, close to forty years earlier.

Though some might wonder about secrets, I know Mom's life was devoted— rarely leaving home, staying at home day and night, no extra money or trips, faithful to marriage and family. In fact, I do not remember one night she went out on the town or was away from home without us.

Their rare outings came after the children left, post-church dinners and dog races. They were all-in for us.

The Third Miracle: A Return of Faithful Love

When Love Crossed Heaven's Gate to Comfort One Last Time.

After her burial, my father, a man of few words and steadfast faith, shared an astonishing revelation.

Approximately three weeks later, my mother returned to him in physical form, with a surrounding glowing divine light, staying for one week to assure him he would be cared for. She spoke with a voice pure as God's — their consciousness connected, and at times they talked to each other. She lay beside him at night and departed peacefully, opening the front door handle and walking down the road.

In hindsight, my father joked that he wished he had taken her to the casino.

This sacred visitation, a testament to their unbreakable love, was not to warn or admonish but to envelop him in love, one more time.

PART IV
The Light That Remains

What My Mom Taught Me About the Power of Prayer and Faith

Lessons of Devotion, Sacrifice, and the Eternal Promise of God's Love

The miracles she left behind are anchors of hope, reminding us that love transcends even death. They whisper of a Heaven where gates swing open, where songs reach God's ears, and where love is so powerful that one may return from eternity to comfort those left behind. My mom instilled prayers like
"Hail Mary,"
"Our Father,"
 "Glory Be,"
 "Act of Contrition",
 "Angel of God," and the Rosary.

We attended church every Sunday
and Holy Day, celebrated Christmas with
songs, family, food, gifts, and an
Advent wreath.
    She sacrificed for Lent and passionately
opposed abortion, with refrigerator magnets
proclaiming
"Who Will Speak Up For the Little Ones."
and
"Abortion kills a BABY every 24 seconds."
The actual magnets are below and are still
on the refrigerator.

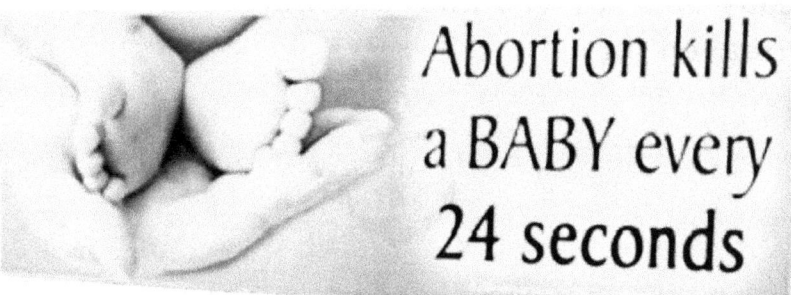

Her faith, rooted in experience as a single mother, reflected her reverence for life. She bought many dolls for her girls, collected some, and adored babies and grandchildren.

Gentle, never raising a fist or cursing, she lived without material wealth, requesting to be buried in a sweatshirt I made bearing her children's names. A symbol of her heart's devotion.

She always prayed to depart before any child, a prayer answered.

I've witnessed personal miracles before and after her passing, perhaps divine preparation—God has a humorous way.

Her three miracles anchor me through challenges. Now, after nearly two decades, I share this in the hope of strength and comfort in loss.

May one day you find love worth leaving Heaven for.

Thoughts and Miracle Meanings I Have Reflected Upon

Reflections on Heaven's signs--and Finding a Love Worth Leaving Heaven For.

Reflecting warmly on these miracles:

The Closet Noise: God delights in Christian music, singing praise, and voices lifted together in love. He uses thunder to proclaim His presence, a loving roar of affirmation.

Hand Swinging Open the Gate: The gate wasn't automatic—she asked humbly.

Heaven's gate exists—although closed, guarding something sacred beyond. Her soul and spirit were welcomed in before her body rested.

Mom's Resurrection: She returned beyond the gate, affirming eternal life. She came back for her love—God and Jesus permitted it. Not for her children, but her husband, with a God-like voice, yet her body and spirit
enveloped in light. Her message was pure love and care, peaceful and wordless at times.

She opened doors like a human, without condemnation, warnings, or future glimpses.

Jesus is love. The Resurrection is true. My mother's faithful life, grounded in faith and family, teaches that we are cherished beyond measure.

May her story inspire you to find one love worth leaving Heaven for, and may her legacy of faith guide you to the eternal embrace of God's grace.

My mom taught us that faith is not just a belief; it's a way of living that echoes into eternity.

If Heaven ever opens its gate again, I know she'll be waiting—smiling, radiant, and ready to say,

"Welcome home, my child."

Prayers We Were Taught

Our Father

Our Father, Who art in Heaven, hallowed be Thy name; Thy Kingdom come, Thy will be done on earth as it is in Heaven. Give us this day our daily bread; and forgive us our trespasses as we forgive those who trespass against us; and lead us not into temptation, but deliver us from evil. Amen.

Hail Mary

Hail Mary full of Grace, the Lord is with thee.
Blessed are thou amongst women and blessed is the fruit of thy womb Jesus.
Holy Mary Mother of God,
pray for us sinners now and at the hour of our death
Amen.

Act of Contrition

O my God, I am heartily sorry for having offended You and I detest all my sins, against thy just punishment, but most of all because they offend you, my God, who are all good and deserving of all my love. I firmly resolve, with the help of your grace, to sin no more and to avoid the near occasion of sin, Amen.

Prayers We Were Taught

Glory Be to the Father

Glory be to the Father and to the Son and to the Holy Spirit. As it was in the beginning is now, and ever shall be, world without end. Amen.

Hail Holy Queen

Hail, holy Queen,
Mother of mercy,
our life, our sweetness and our hope.
To thee do we cry,
poor banished children of Eve:
to thee do we send up our sighs,
mourning and weeping in this valley of tears.
Turn then, most gracious advocate,
thine eyes of mercy toward us,
and after this our exile,
show unto us the blessed fruit of thy womb, Jesus,
O clement, O loving,
O sweet Virgin Mary!
Amen

Angel of God

Angel of God, my Guardian dear, to whom God's love commits me here, ever this day (or night) be at my side, to light and guard, to rule and guide. Amen.

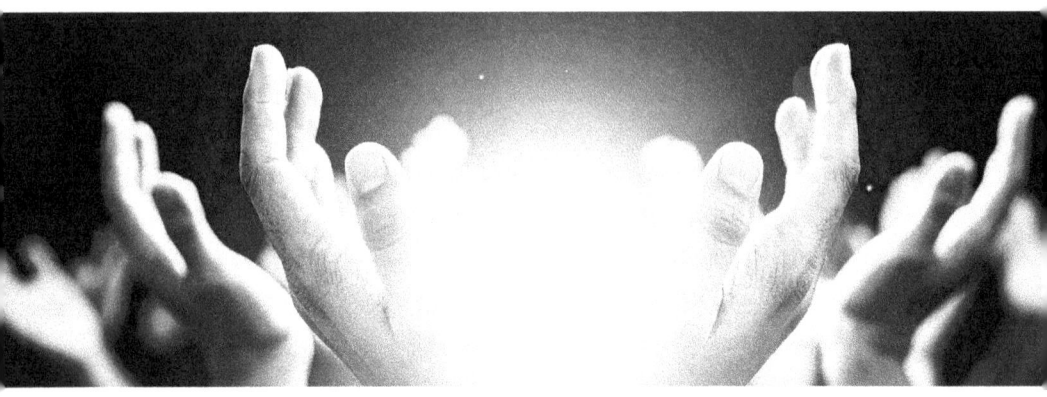

Believe in Miracles

For the latest short true stories visit MiracleAnchor.com.

We accept your true stories as well! If your story is selected we will work with you on the publishing! All true stories have a verification procedure. Evidence is required. We can keep you anonymous as well.

www.ingramcontent.com/pod-product-compliance
Lightning Source LLC
Chambersburg PA
CBHW051712090426
42736CB00013B/2664